A
TESTIMONY
OF FAITH

A
TESTIMONY
OF FAITH

Nancy E. Willard

XULON PRESS

Xulon Press
2301 Lucien Way #415
Maitland, FL 32751
407.339.4217
www.xulonpress.com

Xulon
PRESS

Paperback ISBN-13: 978-1-66284-548-2
Hard Cover ISBN-13: 978-1-66284-549-9
Ebook ISBN-13: 978-1-66284-550-5

TABLE OF CONTENTS

OH, MARY PUREST VIRGIN

Dearest and sweetest Mary, Mother of all roses
In whose Immaculate Heart my own heart reposes
While lying still yet in fervent prayer immersed
I fly to You, my Mother to your beckoned call first
Please call me back then to sanctity without fear
Because your solace and comfort I wish to hear
To hear your voice as shepherdess—call me home
Never, ever to lose sight of You and never to roam
I have wondered far from you, before without intent
Suffering greatly in fear and in hours of discontent
Then by God's grace my composure is renewed
Because I prayed to the Holy Spirit and knew
My Comforter most Holy and Physician divine
Has caused my heart and soul to rest and recline
Please incline Your ears to my intentions pure
And restore my peace of mind to what is secure
I do not take security for granted or ever lose sight
Of the gifts you promise when engaged in a fight
Defining the good and bad in a horrific war
Either to be swallowed up by evil or forever to adore
Jesus' Sacred Heart without hesitancy or pride
For in His Heart is where the confident reside
Live in me, then, Jesus with Your Mother as well
To rise above this evil torment and lonely cell
Imprisoned I am often when temptation arises
Because unity of heart and soul—Satan despises
Yet despite his advances and attacks so bold
You and Mary always bring us back to the fold
Then I shall again fold my hands in prayer for grace
To be restored to sanity and drive Satan to his place

Let all those he tries to devour remain forever aware
Thwart his plans immediately and be prepared
For we know not when the thief comes at night
But when endowed by grace—evil takes flight
So, again Mary, --my fortress and hope
Embrace me in Your arms and help me to cope
Because without You –I know that evil exists
And within Your Beautiful Heart –salvation consists

Written by:
Nancy E. Willard
March 28, 2017

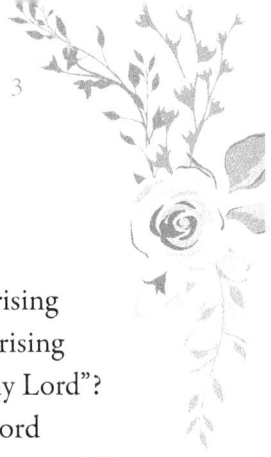

MY TRIUMPHANT LORD

Oh, dearest Jesus, on Easter morn we rejoice in Your rising
As Mary Magdalen discovered an empty tomb so surprising
She exclaimed in astonishment "where have they taken my Lord"?
And discovering Jesus missing could give rise to discord
Then from a distance a voice was heard asking "Whom do you seek"?
Rabboni, Mary said and Jesus began to speak
Do not touch Me for I have not yet ascended to My glory
To be with My Father in heaven—the greatest love story
Doesn't it make one feel the intensity of love Father and Son share
To be in full agreement and bring about salvation to man and spare
Spare the world lost by original sin while out of grace
By an unselfish act of love redeeming mankind to a place
A place called heaven as the Father knows the plan
The plan of salvation available to each woman and man
Just as paradise was lost by disobedience and pride
Satan tempted Eve with cunning and helped her decide
Believing the lie that she and Adam would become like gods
When partaking of the fruit did indeed put them at odds
Oddly enough, though, with paradise lost
A debt was incurred at a very high cost
Costing Jesus His life as a ransom for a debt He didn't owe
Yet He paid with His life so cruelly so that we would know
Know that love always conquers evil when put to the test
Because God prunes us for our good and He knows best
Can we not, then, give Jesus our steadfast attention
Attending the needs of others without mention
Dare we speak of charity and sacrifice as the golden rule
And proclaim justice and equality to all without ridicule
Ridiculous, then, it would be to go against God's will
Because His plan for salvation is greater still

His mercy is coupled with justice at every turn
And turning our lives over to Him, He will not spurn
You see He gives us so many chances to get it right
By following Jesus' example with victory in sight
Victorious then, once more at Easter's dawn
Jesus rose triumphant with all conclusions drawn
Draw closer, then, to Jesus every day
Because He is the Truth, the Life and the Way
Narrow is the gate that leads to heaven it's true
Be vigilant and ever aware that one can misconstrue
Making the mistake of thinking that good works alone can gain
Gain entry into heaven much to our disdain
You see our eternal reward rests upon God's gift
So let's act with prudence and let our voices lift
Lift high to the heavens where choirs of angels sing
Songs of praise and jubilation to Jesus do we bring

Written by:
Nancy E. Willard
April 8, 2017

WE MUST ALWAYS GIVE GOD FIRST PLACE

Of all life's lessons from which one can learn
Can come by prayer and the power to discern
In discovering God's spirit takes fortitude and belief
Depending upon faith for direction and relief
Relief in the sense that we're not alone
Yet together we're part of God's plan that He has shown
That uniting ourselves to Jesus and embrace
Guarantees a relationship with Him by grace
With grace as our shield and personal guide
We can accomplish God's will at every side
So siding in with God takes total surrender, indeed
Allowing ourselves to follow the Shepherd who leads
Leading us home being safe and secure
In verdant pastures, in repose, for sure
In blessed assurance we follow in haste
To our Leader and Our Master—our rightful place
Yes, placing ourselves in His Hands and His Feet
Is the place of ultimate joy as we greet
Greet Jesus as Redeemer and Healer, all in one
United in love to His Heart by compassion won
Winning salvation and peace not known before
A trophy we gain through a cross that He bore
Bearing for us our sins in an effort to erase
To create a clean slate without sin or its trace
When Jesus traced in the sand amongst the people there
His message was clear and they were made aware
Aware that Jesus knew their thoughts inside
And one by one they had to decide

Make a decision based on the truth revealed
By this revelation nothing more was concealed
So when faced with truth, hid not your face
Rather run victorious to the end of the race
In stride, then, walk humbly with your Lord
And avoid all disenchantment and discord
Because to be a noble warrior for God to lead
Takes our willingness and fiat in order to succeed
Successful in our attempt to give God glory
Glory be to God—our greatest love story
As the story is told time after time let us not waste
Waste any time longer to move forward with God at His pace

Written by:
Nancy E. Willard
May 22, 2017

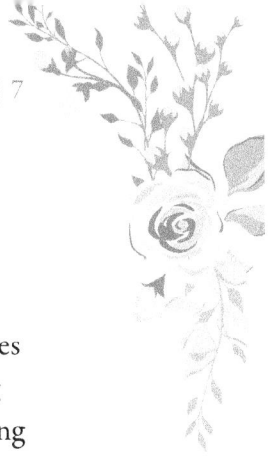

FROM GRIEF TO PEACE

One must grieve before we come to believe
Believing that death brings us to a place that relieves
Relieves the sorrow that we feel in the beginning
By beginning to surrender for a cause we are winning
Then we begin to love and feel whole once more
As we come to accept the joy which He alone restores
Against all odds – we are created anew
Being newly restored to a peace That God renews
Then in gratitude to Him our prayer of thanks we hold
Holding close to our hearts the love that enfolds
Enfolding our hearts with an unknown measure of love
Because love always returns to Heaven above
Hold steadfast, then, to this new place of peace
And our grief and our sorrow are soon released
After being released from this horrible state
One now is whole again and begins to relate
Relating and knowing that our loved ones are now free
Which frees our state of mind, heart and soul – you see
Seeing through the eyes of joy and gratitude
While being grateful gives us a new attitude
Now with a renewed mind we can once again feel
Feeling alive and well – a peace no one can steal
Stealing Heaven like the thief on the cross
By crossing the goal, we are no longer lost
In losing our previous hurts and sorrow that we felt
We now have hope because we have already dealt
Having dealt with the loneliness we once knew
Knowing full well – that God's grace us new
Newly experiencing a zest for life and a burst of strength
Which enables us to move forward and go to any length

So, accept the challenge that He gives us and be aware
That peace comes to those who know God and that He cares
Caring for our souls and for our hearts with our permission
As we surrender our grief without condition
Conditioning and grooming every hair on our head
Giving our lives a new lease on life – instead
Instead of tears, now, we walk in His way
Enfolded in His arms we are invited to stay
So, embrace His love always given as a free gift
And you'll experience a peace that uplifts
By lifting up your life high – comes from God above
Above all else, then, you are free again to love

Written by:
Nancy E. Willard
June 22, 2017

THE CHOICE IS UP TO YOU

Did you know that to be happy is a choice?
In choosing happiness we can rejoice
Rejoice in the fact that our destiny is set
Set by the choices we make without regret
In regretting our decisions is proof of remorse
Because divided by intent we can't stay on course
Of course we can change the decisions we make
By making our situation positive and able to partake
Partake in our life by a glass that is half full
Fulfilling our goal successfully and to pull
Pull all together all the necessary components and rest
Rest in the fact that true effort brings out the best
You see the quality of life depends on right thought
By thinking good thoughts is a sure way to face our lot
And a lot of our happiness results in giving way
To surrender to our God and not to betray
Or be sabotaged by delusions or false intent
Because delusional thinking causes us to repent
Repentance, indeed, can be good for the soul
Because our soul searching pays back double-fold
Enabling us to survive and often see with clarity for sure
Sure of the fact that survival often means to endure
By endurance, then, we can fight the good fight
And accept God's will for us and do what's right
To rightfully own up to responsibility and to trust
Trust in the fact that our positive attitude is a must
Must we become victims swallowed up by depression?
Which causes us grief and sorrow while leaving an impression
That all is hopeless and not possible to find some release
Be released from tragedy and fear which can increase

Increase our failure to think positively and clearly
Clearly we feel doom and pay for it very dearly
Because the negative thinking that we hold in our mind
Gives rise to a place called nowhere which is most unkind
Imprisoned in loneliness and discouragement we flee
Exhausted by our efforts yet yearning to be free
But by courage and the willingness to change our fate
Results in the ability to recognize and relate
Relate to the truth that the choice is ours to make
By making permanent changes and to avoid the mistake
Mistakenly thinking that our fate is sealed
Without escape or the ability to be healed
Healing, then, will always and forever change
Change our course in life and allow us to exchange
By trading off hopelessness and to build upon strength
That same kind of strength can go to much length
To survive the odds and to trust God and really believe
That honest hard work is the reason we achieve
We must not wallow in error that our fate is sealed
Without escape or the ability to be healed
Healing, then, will always and forever make us better women and men
Because in God's grace we find holiness that He extends
So, you alone must make a choice within
To weigh both sides and decide where to begin
Begin to act positively with a newly found freedom won
Because a win always results in the race we have run

Written by:
Nancy E. Willard
July 11, 2017

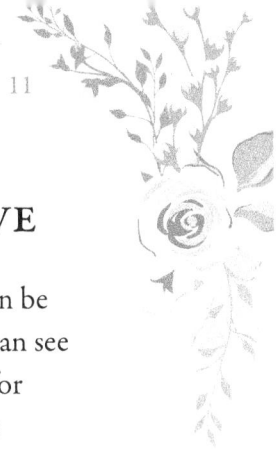

THE MAGNIFICENCE OF LOVE

One can not help but notice how infectious love can be
It starts with simple, little gestures that only the eye can see
With a vision to encounter what we're yearning for
To nourish and to cherish that person we adore
Adoration then elevates one to a higher level of esteem
While becoming aware of the qualities that often redeem
So as beauty is captured within the glance of an eye
We picture our beloved on a pedestal that is set high
Neither height nor length can suitably define this feeling
Because all words fail to describe what is appealing
Can we not, then, appeal to our senses and values that we hold
Holding steadfastly to our values as precious as is gold
Indeed love increases when trust is paramount
Because in sharing one's inner self is really all that counts
Yet not counting the cost of sacrifice—we give with all our hearts
Isn't heartfelt love the message we wish to impart?
What, then, flows from the heart that loves much
Is often the result of kind words or a tender touch
Holding on with gentility and a purpose more intense
Gives rise to harmony and pleasure as well as true recompense
Then being compensated we hold dear to our hearts as well
The endearing qualities that nurture and indwell
A dwelling place, then, that is fitting to those who believe
That love is God-given and it's up to us to receive
Partaking in the sumptuous meal of grace
Set aside for each of us only to be embraced
So never take for granted the love that we can share
And recognize that all other emotions can not compare
To the beauty and magnificence of love mutually expressed
By the words we speak with love, we truly will be blessed

In heaven's choir, then, let's lift our voices high
And sing of love eternal—a joy we can't deny
Because love will always conquer and stand the test of time
To bring us all blessed assurance and a peace that 's truly sublime
Finally, then, with pure intention speak of love often and clearly
And you will be held in high esteem and remembered ever so dearly

Written by:
Nancy E. Willard
July 18, 2017

TAKE ME LORD

When in my silence I ponder awhile
And I consider how often that you are defiled
Being received unworthily without thought
Oh, what bitter consequences this has wrought
May I become willing to suffer for Thee
Take me Lord

When on my knees which seldom is enough
I think of You in Gethsemane and how rough
Difficult for You to witness all our sins in view
While seeing and knowing the cost that was due
Can I share Your ransom for the debt that You paid
Take me Lord

When waking from my night's slumber do I think of You first
To greet my best friend and realize your worth
Unworthy am I, Lord, yet You take me under Your wing
To love and support me in every good thing
In truest appreciation and heartfelt loyalty for Thee
Take me Lord

When starting my day am I aware that You are by my side
Can others see You in me and with me abide
Bidding me well for the peace I wish to share
Sharing with all whom I meet without compare
Only You can change the hearts of mankind
Take me Lord

When I take time for nourishment do I say grace
To thank Thee Lord for my sustenance and embrace
Embrace the fact that You keep me alive and well
Not only in body and mind but also in soul You dwell
May You remain in my heart, too, I plead
Take me Lord

When coming to the end of the day do I respect
And remember my words, actions and deeds and did I reflect
Reflect upon how well or how poorly I treated my fellow man
And was I ready to lend to all a helping hand
Then, Jesus, hand over to me Thy wounds that You bear
Take me Lord
When all is said and done and judgment is what I face
Will I be elected with those who will meet You in Your place
This place is called Heaven where eternity exists
May I hear Your voice, My Good Shepherd and do not resist
So, Lord, I willingly abandon myself to You
Take Me Lord

Written by:
Nancy E. Willard
July 22, 2017

LET YOUR VOICE BE HEARD

When standing up for justice don't be afraid
To speak openly and honestly and don't feel betrayed
If others turn against you and protest what you say
Speak loudly and clearly and in truth all the way
Wayward we become if we don't hold on to our ideals
Because settling for less usually conceals
Hiding from the fact that truth brings about dissention
Dividing and twisting the truth is Satan's intention
Can we just stand by and be led by the masses
Or vote without conscience at every law that passes
Silence and indifference are two great faults
Giving rise to rebellion, crime and assault
Criminal minds, indeed, plot evil and resist
By resisting law and order they easily dismiss
Forgetting that complacence is a worse enemy still
And apathy joins hands which further instills
A pattern of dysfunction passed on to our young
As these children have no clue what has begun
The beginning, then, of turning things around
Takes courage, bravery and truth that resounds
You see, the sounds of silence give way to laws broken
Breaking the hearts of those who have never spoken
Speechless are the unborn whose lives are snuffed out
By the tyranny of abortion we hear children shout
These children could have been our hope and our chance
To bring about change to our world and enhance
To be the voices of truth and not be disturbed
Or denied liberty and freedom which is totally absurd
By starting with one voice invoking God's aid
Will aid and abet the right choices to be made

Don't fear to speak up against evil and crime
Because young babies need not die before their time
Yes, timing is of the essence when the occasion arises
Stand up and be heard with no compromises
Promise to always defend life from beginning to end
And end the silent threat to life that our culture intends
With good intention, then, be heard loud and clear
Because justice always prevails above all our fears
Therefore, the truth always spoken will set the world free
Let it be expressed openly and honestly for all to hear and see

Written by:
Nancy E. Willard
July 22, 2017

HEAVEN'S REHEARSAL

Did you ever consider that life on this earth is a test
Testing our weaknesses and our strengths to do our best
By putting our best foot forward ensures progress
Progressing in right action which deems success
Successfully achieving positive results which leads to a goal
While scoring big time results in a joy to behold
This joy in turn radiates into love and pleasure
Pleasing the heart and soul beyond measure
Then we can be measured by our state of mind as well
To welcome the happiness that heaven foretells
But what happens to the one who refuses to grow
While growing in despair—negativity then flows
This process of decline gives way to depression too
And in depression we don't know what to say or do
We become stunted and limited in limbo as a result
Resulting in broken dreams which make it difficult
The difficulty is in faltering to distinguish what's right and worthwhile
Are we worthy, then, to stand up rather than to live in denial
Can we be denied the help which grace always brings
Because denial of grace closes the door to everything
In every circumstance, then, weigh both sides fairly
And you will not fail—at least fail rarely
Rarely then, do we find true happiness without God's intervention
As He leads us and guides us to good intentions
Intentionally then, choose happiness as your right
Then rightfully so you can move forward with delight
So be pleased to discover that heaven is within reach
Reach out in faith and through your prayer—beseech
Ask God to place heaven in your heart
Because a heart full of love is a wonderful start

In starting over with firm intention and belief
Brings progress in healing and bodily relief
Relieving pain and stress, then, must be our intent
Intentionally choosing to be happy and content
A bone of contention arises, then, when choosing to do wrong
Wrongfully hurting others by judging where they belong
In judgment we shall stand some day with God as our Head
Have we lived for Him or chosen hell instead
Instead of pursuing evil—let us choose what is good
And in the final analysis we'll attain what we should

Written by:
Nancy E. Willard
July 24, 2017

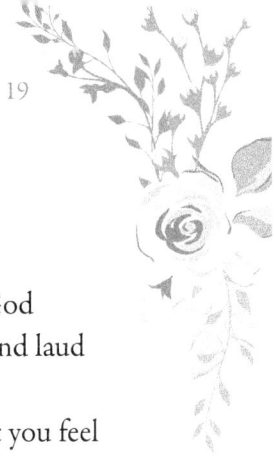

ASPIRING TO POVERTY

P is for the priceless gift of walking humbly with God
O is for the opportunity in prayer to give Him praise and laud
V is for the victory we engaged in a battle real
E is for the emptying of self—surrendering to God what you feel
R is for the ransom that Jesus paid on the cross for all
T is for the truth and loyalty we owe Him as He calls
Y is for the yearning to please God in all things
Isn't poverty, then, a call and answer to all suffering
You see poverty is not a bad thing rather it is a vow instead
Instead of seeking money we must be by the Spirit led
Those called then, are not only vowing poverty but chastity, too
Indeed, chastity happens to be the "pearl" that God is due
In due time, we thirdly promise obedience once more
Because often by obedience we become holier than before
So, before we seek money, fortune and fame
Is really being famous the reason Jesus came?
He was not born in a lofty palace—although He was a king
And that kingdom which He spoke of encompasses everything
We are called also to simplicity of mind and heart
With heartfelt adoration—we set Him apart
Apart from the lure of money exchanged in God's place
Do we not place ourselves in danger in a church we disgrace?
Disgrace and disregard are two of the greatest follies on earth
And Jesus knew that His Father's house was precious and worth
So worthy of the simplest and best feelings we can give
By our giving Him our hearts for as long as we live
So, living in the present moment is what God asks us to do
Don't linger in the past or anticipate the future for you
God's timing, then, for everything is perfect and clear
Clearly requiring our "fiat" as we hold Mary dear

Dearest Mary as your heart is proven forever humble
Help me to give God all of myself and not stumble
Let me not fall into the lure of money and wealth
Because wealth often brings greed and harm to oneself
Can we be selfless stewards of the money that God provides?
It has been proven that we cannot serve two masters--they don't coincide
But never hold back your money from those in need
Poverty is so very real and must be met to feed
To shelter the homeless and free the slaves
To visit the sick and announce that Jesus saves
As my Savior, Jesus, please employ me here and now
To bring about your mission and with charity somehow
Then rich we will all be when we sacrifice much
Not ever counting the cost or the hearts we can touch

Written by:
Nancy E. Willard
July 30, 2017

LOOK TO THE STARS

The light in one's eyes are like a twinkling star
Which brightens the sky so near and so far
The numerous stars in the universe are indeed vast
And we'll never understand why time travels so fast
Why do we hurry so to achieve success?
Does success really measure for us what is best?
To be the best that we can be sometimes brings unhealthy pressure
Because pressure becomes force which shouldn't be measured
You see the true measure of all is in our response to God's will
To be willing to conform our lives to His presence while remaining still
Being still in Him we soon will hear His voice
Telling of His love for us—we can rejoice
Rejoice in the fact that our lives really matter
Not just by matter of fact He calls us to gather
A gathering for His people in a place called His Church
Which remains militant, suffering and triumphant—not rehearsed
There's no room for pretense in the walls of these hallowed places
Because in placing our lives in His hands also replaces
Replaces the loneliness in life as well as the dryness of soul
Which quenches our thirst and fills every hole
Then holy we become because we've opened our minds and hearts
While giving God His due—He now sets us apart
Apart from those who do not honor or revere His name
But rather believing that God is dead—that is their claim
Can we submit to such injustice and what this tyranny brings?
By being lukewarm and silent to everything
Silence can be deadly resulting in apathy for sure
Surely then indifference follows and hinders a cure
We're blinded to the truth that God wishes us to see
Will you close your eyes, too, or will you review openly?

Will you take in all of God's words to heart and to prayer as well?
Then expect that all will be well with our soul and mind to tell
So be mindful of our duties and the effort that it entails
And remain committed because consistency never fails
In failing to look up to the light will bring darkness and delusion
Yes, this delusion only brings us to further confusion
Can we not replace confusion with confession instead?
Because in discovering forgiveness we can hold up our heads
United, then in head, heart and voice we can join together
And discover all the stars in Heaven because we chose the better
Strive, then to be our best and always call for help from the Lord
Because discouragement and failure we simply can't afford
Let us spend, then, our eternity by the way we love and live
And surely as God forgives us we in turn can forgive
We mustn't thank our lucky stars, then, but we must thank God above
Because by reflecting our gratitude we can be seen in the star of love

Written by:
Nancy E. Willard
August 1, 2017

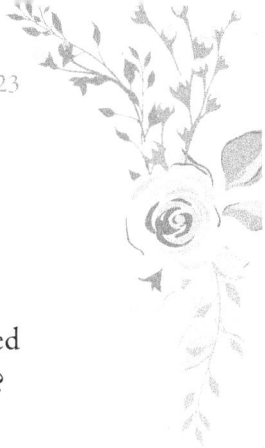

A FRIENDSHIP BLESSED

As written in the Bible—a friend is a treasure
Because in treasuring a friend brings joy unmeasured
Can we measure the depth of the joy that we feel?
I think not because this emotion reveals
A revelation that heaven has come down to earth
As revealed in and through Christ we are made aware of His worth
Are we worthy of partaking in this sacred bond?
Bonding in love together as He calls us to respond
Responding yes, Lord, I offer my life to You
Will You take my love, heart and soul and review
Taking all into consideration (mostly take my heart)
Set it apart from the world and let me start
Starting each day with the first thought of You, Lord
Knowing full well that Your richness I can't afford
Yet how priceless it is to desire your wealth
While emptying myself I come to true health
Healthy, indeed, and refreshed in body for sure
I'm sure that Your love always brings a cure
Curing mind, body and soul with a purpose to grow
Grow in affection for You is all we need to know
Knowing full well that this love is sufficient
Because all other love is not whole and efficient
Only Your love is lasting Lord—as You reveal
By revealing Yourself invites reciprocity and true appeal
By appealing to our senses, You set in motion
Enabling us to move closer to You with high emotions
Our feelings become blessed in revering Your name
Because by adoring You in the Tabernacle, we're never the same
Yet being forever changed we should remain steadfast
Because love for Thee, Lord will forever last

A lasting, life-long union of friendship shared
In sharing a reciprocal bond, we become aware
Aware of the fact that nothing else matters
Let us not lose this resolve or become scattered
Let us then scatter the seeds of love wherever we go
Going confidently forward with that love which continues to grow
Growing day by day—each soul at a time
And timing is all important—just like poetry rhymes
Let us practice and rehearse this wonderful ending
Which remains eternal for all without pretending
Do not pretend in this relationship so dear
Because by giving our love completely we have nothing to fear
Fear not, then, to tread the waters and cross
Cross over to paradise and you'll never be lost
Because in losing oneself we gain so much more
As matched by our willingness to seek and explore
By exploration, then we find a treasure to behold
By our total acceptance and surrender of our souls
Invites the Heart of Jesus to not only open but to also console
In consolation, then, let us remain steadfast
By heeding God's call to a vocation that lasts
By heeding His call, we partake in a blessed friendship forever to be
If we just say "yes", give thanks, and always agree
Agree to serve Him alone as our truest endeavor
Which will guarantee our eternity in heaven with Him forever

Written by:
Nancy E. Willard
August 8, 2017

THE NECESSITY OF PRAYER

To offer ourselves up to God in prayer is the highest form of praise
Because it is a perfect way to end and to start each day
It is true that daily we have a cross to bear
And Jesus calls us to surrender to Him our every care
Do we care enough for God and others to love as much
To tenderly call God-Father-and receive His touch
His touch is so gentle, so loving and so true
In true partnership, then, He calls us to renew
To renew our baptismal vows as a true sign of our calling
Being called upon to serve Him alone without falling
Falling into the trap of pride—the trick that always deceives
Creating an allurement of power yet the opposite we receive
Yet in realizing our powerlessness we soon find
That God is our power, glory and kingdom to all mankind
So, to address God in daily prayer results in forming a bond
Bonding heart to heart feelings that become deep and fond
Haven't we all in fond memory been touched by His grace
When He has offered us His solace and tender embrace
We all need to cling to Him and to heed His constant plea
Stay close to me child, take on my Yoke and follow Me
How much clearer can God be when asking us to follow His will
Do we willingly follow or do we hesitate still
Yet in total stillness we can begin to experience our Maker
Wouldn't it be foolishness and folly not to be a partaker
To become a part of a lively and eternal peace
And in and through this unity all wars would cease
With peace, then as our aim pray with all your heart
Unite it to your mind and soul for a start
As you begin each day thank the Lord with sincerity
And He will reward you with His peace and clarity

Clearly, then, talk to God, as you would to your most cherished friend
And He will double your joy and always extend
Extend His loving arms around you so warm and tight
And you'll discover that His Perfect love is so right
It is right then to daily perform the practice of prayer and kneel
Kneeling before Him in adoration He can't conceal
Conceal His utmost love reserved especially for you
Then having been made aware of His love—heaven becomes true
Be true to thyself, then, and surely you can expect
Expect a miracle from the God whom you honestly respect

Written by:
Nancy E. Willard
August 11, 2017

COMMON SENSE – A LOST ART

Right thinking is a process of deliberation
As well as a positive attitude
Because being positive sets in motion
A path that is clear which is common sense
Clearly, then, you get out of life
Just what you put into it
When you absorb the good
You will feel exhilarated and joyful
When you absorb the bad
You will feel abandoned and hateful
When caught up in this incredible turmoil
Do we succumb and become too tired to fight?
Or do we look upward and pray with all our might
Might we often miss out on those heavenly graces
That allow us to feel God and experience His embraces
So, embrace Him and seize the moment when help is near
Because near to God is a place that we should never fear
Yet without faith--fear can often return
This is when we must surrender and allow our hearts to burn
To be set afire once more by the Holy Spirit divine
Because divine Intervention wins out every time
In time, then, when we return the favor of love
Truly, we've experienced the Holy Spirit from above
Above all else let us answer the call and complete
Completely trusting in God and His powerful elite
Just who are these elite? they are the angels and saints
Whose lives reflects the artist Creator and what He paints
His art work can't be duplicated in color or hue
Many have tried, unsuccessfully, without a clue
Just as art depicts beauty, poetry as well, reflects

Reflecting the heart of the poet and what to expect
So, expect great things to happen when employing common sense
Because we'll have much in common which will be our recompense
The gift, then, of expression as an art must be
A portrait of the soul, in love, with God you see
So, see to it always to put God first
First, give Him your love spontaneously--not rehearsed
Don't practice your conversation but pray openly
Because He delights to receive you in every degree
Totally abandon yourself to Him and do not withhold
Your hurts, dreams and the desires of your heart seven-fold
So, remember too, in prayer to include all things
Because He loves it when you ask Him-- His Heart sings
Sing joyfully to the Lord your song of praise
For in praising Him-- choirs join in and raise
They lift up the petitions of a fervent soul
Representing our gift to Jesus, on the Cross--a joy to behold
Just as Jesus said to His Mother, "woman, behold your son"
And to John, "behold your Mother", motherhood began
So, Mary, my Mother, redeem and refresh my common sense
And help me to become worthy of God without pretense

Written by:
Nancy E. Willard
August 21, 2017

Back to Tradition

If faith is understood as a matter for the living
One must live life and be genuinely forgiving
To forgive from the heart calls for loving in return
Not in returning malice but to be willing to discern
Discernment is a necessary process in knowing right from wrong
And by wrongfully judging others just doesn't belong
Yet we all have the need to belong to someone or something
But sometimes we can't accept pain and suffering
All suffering has a purpose to a greater or lesser degree
But no degree is needed when applying common sense can't you see
If seeing is believing we need to be willing to open-up our eyes wide
Widen our perception, see more clearly issues on the other side
Yet by siding-in with the trends of life rather than be counted
Shouldn't it count that problems have to be surmounted
To go beyond—rise up—and let your voices be heard
Because indifference and apathy become absurd
And what is absurdity? It becomes ludicrous and untrue
In truth, then, don't we need to review
Review the values and standards by which we stand for
So, standing up for what is right is not wrong
And by doing wrong increases sin taking us places where we don't belong
A sense of belonging brings people to God seeking relief
Relief from all pain and clinging to some belief
Can't we believe in God, morality and His commands?
To take a commanding lead against the ills that society now demands
Demanding justice and mercy is what Jesus asks
So, ask for these virtues to carry out His task
This task is our duty and God-given right
Rightfully, so, let's pursue this cause with all our might
Almighty, then, is our God, Creator and Judge

And judging from the standards of today—we all need a nudge
A gentle push in the direction of wisdom and courage
The courage to change to the positive and not to discourage
Discouragement is found when down and out, without hope
Hope cannot be abandoned when seeking a means and ability to cope
To meet with and deal with problems head on
Is so necessary to being healthy and strong
Then, may I strongly suggest resurrecting tradition and what it stands for?
Don't stand idly by when virtue is needed
Rather show the need for values to be heeded
Again, take heed in this suggestion and pray for change
Change the course of history and seek to arrange
To place and order a plan-- a method to invent
Because Divine intervention is the only way to true content
So, true contentment, takes commitment and trust
By trusting in instinct and in survival is a must
Must we continue to watch so many die
Die by abortion, war and assisted suicide—can we stand by?
If idleness is the playground in which Satan works
Work to thwart his plans and his preposterous quirks
Turn away from the evil He plots to put into your mind
Being mindful of the fact that he seeks to undermine
To weaken the solid foundation of God's Holy Church
So, attend church faithfully and you won't have to search
Look to the Bible and remember the verses that you read
By seeking God, first, all else will follow in all of your needs
Remember the needy, too, for truly God's kingdom is theirs
Like the beatitude claims—they are the heirs
To be heirs as well is not impossible or remote
I have aired my views, in an effort to promote
To raise an awareness that a decline of respect, in God's house, is on the rise
Will you rise up and return to proper dresses and suits and ties?
This ties in with reverence for God and His holy place

So, God has placed upon us a free will and grace
That grace being sufficient, when at Mass we receive
Receive Jesus' Body and Blood—what a joy to perceive
Let's take note to receive Him properly—oh, we should receive Him on
bended knee
Kneeling in respect and gratitude-- should be our heart's serenity
So, put in order, once more, the reverence due God within His walls
Because His walls belong to His Bride—the Catholic Church after all
With all these ideas—let us ponder upon them with zeal
Because God loves zealous laborers in His vineyards for real

Written by:
Nancy E. Willard
August 29, 2017

DISCIPLESHIP OR DISTRACTION

Do you know that discipleship calls for discipline of the will
Willing to follow Jesus and His teaching until
Until and when we surrender to His ways and believe
Believe that His intention is to give-- as we are to receive
He gives us His Heart so Sacred and Divine
And He came down to earth to save humankind
As human beings, then, we are called to become holy and pure
With purity of intention, then we can endure
Endurance takes strength to go that extra mile
Walking in step with God with happiness and a smile
Can we not smile when we encounter love so real
Because in reality love is not meant to be concealed
To hold back love is unnatural for those who are free
There's freedom in bonding in love won't you agree
Agreeing, as Jesus did to put your life on the line
Serving the poor, the lame, the deaf and the blind
Can we be blind to the truth that love can conquer all
With all of our hearts let's move forward and not stumble or fall
Rather let us fall in love with Our Savior and carry our cross
That cross being our ticket to heaven—we'll never be lost
Yet losing our souls is the devil's intent
His intention is wicked and he will not relent
Relentless in nature the devil seeks souls to devour
Like a roaring lion preying on those who cower
He demands us to fear our every thought and move
Causing grief and confusion in order to remove
To intend to steal our innocence and cause us to sin
Falling prey to our passions is when trouble begins
Yet, in the beginning God created day and night
And seeing that it was good became His delight

Should we not take delight that we have a choice
To choose happiness with God and rejoice
Rejoicing in the fact that salvation is at hand
When we hand over ourselves completely and come to understand
Understand that God wants our all without exception
Not to hold back our feelings and intentions
With willful submission to God takes faith indeed
Yet He knows us better than ourselves and what we need
To the needy, the poor and sinners as well
He welcomes us with open arms and then He tells
Speaking to us in the silence of our hearts
With heartfelt love, He seeks to impart
Yes, Jesus' parting words were I will be with you always
Not leaving us as orphans with no place to stay
So, stay and remain steady on your feet
Walk humbly with your God and you will defeat
Defeat the enemy and put evil in its place
While placing our trust in God—someday we'll see His Face
So, face up to discipline and be not distracted
Don't lose your ability to pray and be contacted
We are called to discipleship and to walk in God's ways
Because the ways to salvation comes to those who pray
Pray that you conquer all sin and distress
And you'll find that God alone helps us to peace and rest
So, rest in the arms of a loving God when He calls you
Call Him your own—because He makes all things new

Written by:
Nancy E. Willard
September 2, 2017

FORBEARANCE

One of the most admirable traits we need to reflect upon is self-control
Because forbearance should become our personal goal
To endure pain or just put up with displeasure
Isn't it displeasing to God not to use our own talents and treasures
Find richness in your ability to keep yourself in check
To bring a balance to your life without being a nervous wreck
We all will be reckoned with by the manner in which we live
So, live by God's commandments and be willing to forgive
Forgiveness must come from the will and takes resolve
In resolving to pardon a sin or offense does involve
Which requires a change of heart with mercy as the intention
To intentionally choose forbearance without exception
Neither take offense by nor offend anyone by your vanity
Because in taking God's name in vain can lead to insanity
Therefore, without forbearance, once more we'll find chaos and unrest
Resulting in calumny and becoming distressed
Unable to sustain a balance between right and wrong
Until we feel disoriented or in a place where we don't belong
So, a sense of belonging makes one feel connected
Joined together in a relationship so much better than expected
Do you or can you say that you expect a miracle today?
To discover God's love for you and His purpose for you along the way
And, by the way, don't fall into the trap of doubt and fear
Because by being afraid makes all things unclear
Clearly, then, if we become willing to pray and endure
By enduring in prayer, we have hope to secure
We will be secured a place in heaven with no more pain
Without pain, then, suffering did have its gain
So, isn't it more gainful to forbear without feign
Which gains strength of character and the ability to ordain

To invest in and participate in a purpose worthwhile
Enabling us to say that it was worth the effort to go that extra mile
We must not then take in stride the newly found peace
Because through this discovery of peace we can be released
Would you, dear Lord, sustain me in my every need?
I need You, Lord, take my heart and lead
As I ask of You, to allow me to forbear all that You will
And help me to be willing to love Thee and be spirit-filled

Written by:
Nancy E. Willard
September 10, 2017

Our Lives are a Gift

Can we believe with certainty that life is a gift?
A present from God to whom we should lift
Lift high to heaven the thanks that we feel
And feeling special brings a joy that we can't conceal
So, don't hide your face in shame or fear
Rather invite all into your heart and those you hold dear
Love back in return, your enemies as well
Welcome them, like God welcomes us, does that ring a bell?
Let freedom ring when choosing between the better of two choices
Choosing the positive as spoken in our voices
While voicing your opinion, please, keep it honest
Because honestly, we are called to be simple and modest
Modesty, then, should encourage us to be chaste
And chastity is a virtue we can't afford to waste
Don't waste your time in frivolous matters
As a matter of fact, time wasted, only scatters
A scatterbrain we can all become by time poorly spent
Because lack of discipline causes us to be sorry and repent
Are we truly sorry, or do we learn to become wise?
And by not acting wisely can become our demise
Let's not, then, dismiss fact or even disguise
Or hide from the truth—JUST OPEN YOUR EYES
Please don't lose sight of God, Our Creator who makes
Makes sure that our happiness is always at stake
Let's not make the mistake of being lukewarm and distant
Let's not distant ourselves from God for an instant
Because division can be created by willful pride
Just as the fallen angels chose the other side
Let's not side in with Satan who tries to threaten our free will
Let's rather be willing to accept God's grace in order to be fulfilled

Isn't it fulfilling and humbling to know that God loves us so much?
Let's embrace those moments and keep in touch
In touch with the fact that we're all called to be true
Truthful at all times to those who haven't a clue
That heaven is within you—the GIFT—the surprise
It really shouldn't surprise the humble or the wise
Therefore, true wisdom is God's gift and our cause for rapture
Because by saying "yes" to Him—our souls have been captured

Written by:
Nancy E. Willard
September 12, 2017

TRAPPED IN PERFECTIONISM

It's way too dangerous to make your standards too high
When you get overwhelmed and deny
Deny that being perfect belongs only to God
By playing God is offensive—a road heavily trod
And treading on thin ice invites falling through
Putting you in danger with the need to be rescued
Dangerous it is to dwell in the past as well
Because the past you can't change or in it dwell
When dwelling in the negative we shut out the good
It is good, then, to think positive and be understood
Being understanding with oneself is a challenge indeed
Especially when we're frustrated and in need
And needing help is healthy as well
So, welcome those who help you into your life and excel
To excel, however, beyond the limits that are set
Brings on disappointment and sometimes regret
Regretfully so we're all driven to do our best
But in hindsight isn't it better to rest
Because resting when weary can eliminate stress
And being stressed-out we fail to make progress
If we progress in failure, then, surely, we will suffer
Suffer from increased pain without a buffer
Now exposed to danger and the threat of being hurt
Our defenses go up sharply and we must be alert
Alert to the fact that depression will rear its ugly head
Heading toward withdrawal and anger instead
What feeds this anger, then, comes about by not getting our own way
We've become spoiled and regrettably stay
Stay in a quagmire of sorts or a sensation of drowning
Actually, drowning in self-pity and always frowning

What's the alternative to perfectionism would you say?
One must speak to God in prayer—and He'll lead the way
Why shouldn't we tell Him, Lord—I'm really mad
Mad at the world and feeling really sad
This saddens our Lord when we don't get it right
Because our self-driven nature makes us uptight
So, let go of the grip that perfectionism causes
Take care to stop and think and take frequent pauses
Breathe deeply and slowly and resign to do your best
Because it's better to compete when you've had sufficient rest
So, in the end, don't be restless but cautious and steady
Because steadiness wins out and you'll always be ready
Ready to face, head on, our goals and our dreams
And awaken prepared and filled with a new self-esteem

Written by:
Nancy E. Willard
September 13, 2017

EMPTY YOURSELF FOR ME

It is no secret that we should love God with all our might
Might we, then, take the opportunity to make all things right
We need to empty ourselves in order to be filled
With honest consideration, then, let's do God's will
We must be willing to give to others our all
Giving from our hearts will answering a call
A call to love one another just as Jesus did
Not to judge or speak unkindly—heaven forbid
Indeed, heaven is here—right on this earth
Inclusive for all starting at birth
Then shortly after birth we are baptized and rightfully so
We grow in character and we witness what we know
After a few years, we receive Communion for the first time
As our attitude must be holy and sublime
Because in receiving Christ so adored
Gives way to an experience of right accord
Can we empty ourselves when receiving our King?
On bended knee and with love as our offering
We must have purity of soul as well as a pure heart
With purity of intention, then, we will start
As we begin in our emptiness to be filled with grace
In gratitude, then, we must put God in first place
Can we not place our desires and our hearts at Jesus' feet
Right there at the foot of the Cross—it's Him that we greet
Let's greet Him with reverence and give Him our soul
Because to love Him is the sole purpose of becoming whole
We grow in His likeness and a willingness to please
Until we become one with God—with such ease
Then we are filled, in addition, with holiness and hope
Hoping that God will lead us to a place where we can cope

By our willingness to surrender to God once more
Your will be done becomes more meaningful than before
It pleases God immensely when we sing of Him with praise
When praising God our hearts and spirits are raised
We address Him on high and give God his due
And He will make known the vocation that He chose for you
So, be the best that you can be and always strive
To be grateful for everything, yes, even in being alive
You see each day is a gift to be cherished again and again
Yes, it's good to remember the places that we've been
If we all can offer our sacrifices that we face and feel
While facing up to the truth has so much more appeal
In supplication, then, ask God to fill our needy hearts
To beat steadily in rhythm is exactly how love starts
So, start each day, by emptying yourself for God's sake
And you'll soon discover that God never makes mistakes

Written by:
Nancy E. Willard
September 18, 2017

YOU ARE THE KEY TO MY HEART

Only once in a lifetime do you find a match
One who takes your breath away—it's hard to catch
After catching one's breath, the realization becomes clear
That you love this person whether it be far or near
Being near to you makes all things right
And rightfully so, my heart takes flight
Yes, flighty I can be, but I'll stand my ground
Because I cherish this love I have found
In finding you, I have found myself as well
And all is well with me and in my heart, you dwell
A dwelling place that will always be safe and secure
Because quite frankly it's a place that's pure
With purity of intention, I dare to say
That my God has placed, thee, in my heart to stay
Please don't fear, ever, that this feeling will change
You've changed me, dear, since we've exchanged
Voicing our inner selves to one another—just to be heard
And after having shared this intimacy—a friendship has been secured
Security is and always will be an issue with me
Because to trust anyone is hard you see
Very often I have been hardened by past hurts inside
Inwardly feeling awkward until my fear subsides
Yes, fear can rip your heart apart
When you're lonely and not so smart
So, these words to the wise are to be focused in your mind
Be mindful of the fact that love can make you blind
Blindness is not just physical but spiritual, too
When we catch ourselves trying to stay on cue
Clueless, as well, can we become—next
That we can experience words and feelings out of context

Misunderstanding and real fear becomes the risk
As you question yourself and why you exist
The heart is not meant to be sad or broken
But actions speak louder than words can be spoken
And speaking of hurt reminds us still
That nothing or no one can ever fulfill
Fill the need, inside, to be loved and wanted
When by doubt you are constantly haunted
You, my dear, hold the key to my heart
And our shared respect for each other sets us apart
When separated from you, I carry you inside
Always with the desire to be by your side
And in siding-in with you I've discovered who I am
I am tamed and contented and as gentle as a lamb
And I will not permit Satan to pull the wool over my eyes
Because He seeks to destroy—He's the father of lies
Therefore, I won't lie to you and I'm taking a chance
The chance to tell you that now I can dance
Dance to the beat of an everlasting song
That love is eternal and ever so strong
So, thank you, dear for your love-gifts and power
You exist in my heart every minute and hour
Let's pray, then, that God allows us many years
And to be forever, together, both in happiness and tears
Because tears of joy have become our ebb and tide flowing
With oceans of love that God has been bestowing

Written by:
Nancy E. Willard
September 19, 2017

BID ME TO FOLLOW
YOUR HOLY WILL

Lord, I am thirsty—give me a drink
Of Your ever-lasting water—help me to think
Think thoughts of completely serving You
Because without You—I'd have no purpose, it's true
Clueless, then, must I wander alone
Lost and lonely—for my sins to atone
True sorrow for our sins is necessary for sure
To enable us to find peace and be pure
Purity, then, is the most pleasing to God above
Because those who please Him feel nothing but love
Love is not only a tender word but also a deep feeling
Causing one's heart to flutter which brings about healing
With Jesus, as Lord, He is the Divine Physician
Which sets Him apart as Healer—His truest position
Please point me in a position sincere
When I can give of myself totally, to You, without fear
Fearless, then, I will take on my armor and shield
As a warrior for You as I surrender myself and yield
Yielding to Your will with a purpose and need
Oh, Lord, I need You in order to succeed
Success can only be measured by giving our all
Willingly and tirelessly while answering the call
A call to our vocation—whatever it may be
And just maybe "we'll get it" then we can be set free
Free to love in a way that we couldn't before
With a purpose of peace—Yes, Lord, it's we who adore
Because in adoration, to Thee, we can feel Your embrace
So, we must embrace all whom we meet—yet give them space

Just enough space to enable them to see the other side
Clearly, then, with love in our hearts we can truly abide
Oh, what a feeling we can experience and share
When we experience joy abundantly beyond compare
By comparison, then, the choice is ours to make
Let us choose wisely and not make the same mistakes
Because we have much to gain and little to fear
Be fearless in intention and in purpose clear
Clearly, then, with purpose we have the opportunity to grow
By following God's will we come to know
And you'll feel much better—a kind of peace within
So, be a peacemaker and just watch it begin
Begin to undo the knots that we tie
The, we must pray to Mary—she's very close by
You see, long ago Mary said "yes", Thy will be done
Which set God's plan for salvation—a gift to be won
Let us all become winners—in the places we find
Securing a peace which is gentle and kind
Because kindness, too, calls us to give our all
To all those in need to break down those walls
Take on the challenge of loving with all your might and courage
Yes, brave hearts we'll have with the ability to encourage
Because encouragement becomes our buckler and shield
Especially when it is to humility that we yield
By yielding to God's will with a promise to keep
Keeping in mind that God's love is ever so deep
Yes, the depth of His love is infinite as well
Be it well with our souls when in heaven we dwell
So, diligently seek His kingdom by His grace to sustain
Then, by His side we'll forever remain
Therefore, God's grace is sufficient and real
As He pours into our hearts, the love that He feels
This feeling of awe will sustain us always and forever be

The proof of God's love which holds the eternal key

Written by:
Nancy E. Willard
September 25, 2017

THE ABILITY TO COMPROMISE

To meet someone half way is proper you know
Knowing full well that affection will soon grow
Within each one of us is the ability to be proper and kind
Why not be willing to compromise rather than bind
We're bound to make mistakes for sure
So be aware that kindness will always endure
Endurance is not only fitting but also a call to be
The best in achieving your goal willingly
Don't you know, too, that manners are called for as well
And by welcoming others we indeed can foretell
That the future will hold the answer that we expect
When offering to all your love and respect
Respectfully so show gratitude and kindness too
Because what you do and say will always come back to you
Leading the way to peace and contentment
Why wallow in pride and show resentment
To resent someone shows envy and pride
Should we not take pride and pleasure in seeing the other side
Inside all of us is the need for love and well we need
Need acceptance and affection in order to succeed
Success is not only attainable but it is also a goal to achieve
Again, should we not give of ourselves in order to receive
Take pride, too, in your manner of expression
Because kindness always grows and leaves the impression
Impress upon those who you encounter each day
The necessity to communicate with God and to pray
Prayer is so powerful and can change everything
We must all have faith that prayer can bring
Bring healing and wellness enabling us to be free
That freedom to be the best person that we can be

So, be honest and open with a heart which delights
With arms open wide and the willingness to invite
By invitation for sure, God calls us to a holy place
Why not place our full trust in God with the problems that we face
Because facing up to reality we can't achieve on our own
Unless we are willing to accept and condone
Not upon condition, then, should we limit anyone
Compliment those we love for a job well done
By encouragement as well—we invite joy
So, invite all those around you to use and employ
Working toward your future, your plans and your dreams
Awake from your slumber and hold in esteem
Those people who support you and are willing to show
A place of contentment in which you can grow
Will you stand behind me or be at my side
And bring joy to my heart and with peace abide
Let's agree, then, to love each other and always instill
That in attaining one's goal in life is greater still
So, be still and know that God in silence is there
And He has prepared a place for us beyond compare
So, don't compromise this gift freely given—because He wills
That we graciously accept His will with a love that fulfills
Fulfillment is not compromised when taking a chance
Because chances are what we know can enhance
Find beauty, then, in the simplest of pleasures
And your heart will have found its greatest treasure
So, treasure this love which takes compromise and trust
And be sincere in intention and swallow your pride if you must

Written by:
Nancy E. Willard
September 28, 2017

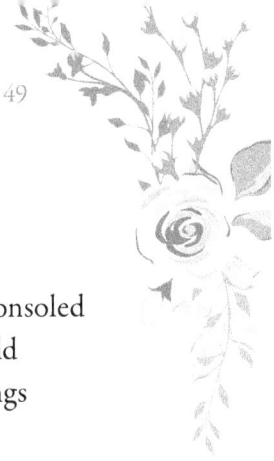

CONSOLATION

Is it not the Franciscan way to console rather than be consoled
Making sure to express your love and not withhold
Because feigning affection and holding back feelings
Impedes growth and the necessity for healing
So always have the right intention to allay grief
And you'll touch the hearts of many while bringing relief
To endeavor to lessen the grief and sorrow
Does in fact increase the chances of facing tomorrow
So, always live in the present—it's really the only time
A time we are given in youth and in our prime
Primarily, then, consolation brings solace and ease
Easing the pain of others and allowing them to seize
Again, seizing the moment is a good practice to follow
Because time always heals the heart that is hollow
Yes, grief causes a gaping hole in the heart when unattended
So, pay attention and accept from others the love that's intended
The best of intentions can fall short it's true
But in truth consolation diminishes the blues
Color your world, then, with acceptance and grace
And you'll find that everything will fall into place
By placing your trials at the foot of the cross
Brings so much consolation to Jesus who suffered loss
Lose yourself in His wounds and ease His pain
Because it was His life that He ransomed for our gain
The good thief on the cross sought consolation as well
Because he saw with his eyes the chance in heaven to dwell
As Jesus told him "you will be in paradise with Me"
Oh, what blessed joy and assurance to follow Thee
We are never alone but our faith must increase
To augment our happiness while giving us peace

This peace so serene and unending for sure
Surely, then, with God's love we can endure
While bearing the pain we can unite
Joining our suffering with Jesus'—He can make all things right
Rightfully, so, always give God His due
And you'll discover that goodness will return to you
By this wonderful exchange, remember to always show gratitude
To be gracious to God with a new attitude
Can we, then, assume a posture of kneeling
On bended knee bring Him honor and feeling
Because adoration belongs to God alone, indeed
Then we can console Him and experience the consolation that we need
After having exchanged this most wonderful feeling we can feel blessed
Because God in His love makes up for the rest
So, rest comfortably in the Lord always and honor His name
And you'll find that your life will never be the same

Written by:
Nancy E. Willard
October 7, 2017

BEAR WITH EACH OTHER'S FAULTS

To love one's neighbor is a command that Jesus said
Don't judge or gossip just to get ahead
Your manner in judging comes out in your speech
Speak well, then, of others and learn to teach
As a teacher instructs his students with deliberate care
Take care to act kindly in all your affairs
Because prudence becomes a trait to acquire
Be intelligent and wise and do what's required
A requirement, therefore, becomes a need
Need we fight or argue and not take heed
Heading for disaster is common when not in tune
And harmony suffers and brings about gloom
Just as skies are gray and clouds are dark
Darkness can overshadow us and leave a mark
Remarks, then, can hurt the one we love by hurt
Let us be careful in speech and be alert
Alert to the fact that kindness is the Spirit's fruit
So be kind in spirit and let love take root
But rooted in pride is a mistake we often make
Make sure that our egos don't cause us to make mistakes
Mistakenly, so, we can, by our example lead others astray
Causing confusion and the ability to lose their way
As we follow a path of doom and gloom
Which causes calamity which gives little room
If we limit or hinder those whom we face
We fail most assuredly and don't give them space
We crowd out their progress in a harmful way
So, bear with one another and for them—pray
Prayer can lift up many a soul
So, kneel and pray sincerely and you"ll receive double-fold

Twice as much harmony will be a result
Resulting in peace—without insults
Insulting it is to be rude and careless
Carelessly judging others with full awareness
Take heed, then, to follow our Lord's command
Do unto others as you should understand
Bearing with one another's faults within reason
Give rise to justice no matter what season
Seasoned we become when following a path
In the direction of love without malice or wrath
You see, anger increases every time we turn inside
On ourselves and others bringing injury and pride
Prideful we become and depressed as well
Because anger turned inward begins to swell
Then increasingly we find ourselves caught in the storm
Which can rain on our parade in every form
So, formulate a pattern of truth and might
Because Almighty God always asks us to do what is right
Rightfully so, bear with patience what we've been told
Be kind in manner and speech so peace can unfold
Then we'll find peace in a way we've never known
Because God's Spirit is in us and He has already shown
Showing that right thought and action becomes the norm
And as a result, many new friendships can be formed
So be attentive and sober and very alert
Alert to the fact that it's others we hurt
When we can't bear, adversity or be willing to live
By a standard of humility—truly we must forgive
Because forgiveness must always remain a two-way street
Which results in victory and not defeat

Written by:
Nancy E. Willard
September 29, 2017

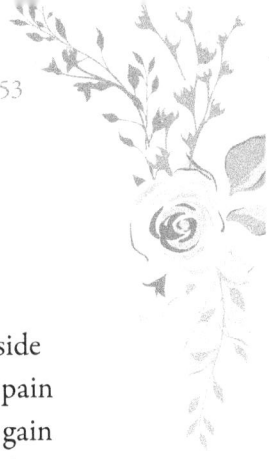

THE DESIRE TO BE HOLY

Those who follow Christ have the spirit inside
To hear Him, to obey Him and within His Heart reside
To also live within His wounds and contemplate His pain
Painful as it may be or seem—you'll have so much to gain
To be gainfully aware that our Lord loves us so much
Not just in word or in deed but by His heavenly touch
With hands outstretched He calls us each by name
If and when we respond to Him—we'll never be the same
This change and transition is not only subtle but is also real
When reality sets in we capture its power with zeal
Yes, to be zealous means that our soul is on fire
Fired up by a purpose to seek and to desire
This search for love must be conscious and be bold
Be audacious, then, and forgive seven-fold
Because forgiveness is the greatest gift that we can receive
So, welcome forgiveness with an aim to always believe
Believe and experience a conversion like never before
Because the best is yet to be in experiencing just what God holds in store
The restoration of our souls is His purpose firm
Be firm and resolve to be changed as well as confirmed
In confirmation, then, we become a witness who is to be
A soldier in faith and to give God our solemn loyalty
In being loyal we promise to renounce evil at every turn
As we vow to a holier life with the ability to discern
Discernment is what the Holy Spirit gives us in order to weigh
To measure the checks and balances that He provides along the way
Truly, the path that we choose and walk by is a matter of choice
And always choosing to do good causes heaven to rejoice
Be glad, too, when our words and efforts aren't enough
Because we can falter and waiver from the truth when the going gets rough

In order to smooth out the defects which can come our way
We must humbly walk with God and pray never to stray
If, perchance, we lose our way—Jesus will set out to find
To seek us out when lost and feeling left behind
So, let's be obedient and answer the call of the Lord
Listen to His voice alone because we can't afford
You see poverty of spirit brings richness as well as healing
And recovery from sickness and pain is very appealing
If we strive toward holiness with heaven as our goal
The end result will be eternal happiness within the fold
Just as the sheep and the goats will be separated at judgment
Let's be judicious in our choices to avoid chastisement
We have nothing to fear, then, if we let holiness bloom
Because in heaven, God has many mansions and makes room
A final dwelling place where peace and harmony will reign
And above all else there'll be no sorrow and love will remain

Written by:
Nancy E. Willard
October 29, 2017

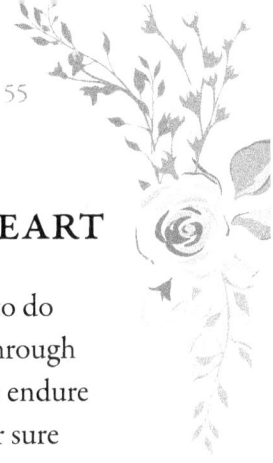

WRITE YOUR LAW UPON MY HEART

To obey You, Oh Almighty God is what you call us to do
By doing Your will obediently You will always see us through
Through the hardships and suffering that we're asked to endure
Can lead us to a worthwhile purpose like holiness for sure
We can't always be sure of the outcome we will face
When facing up to the reality that everything has its place
Just as God places in our lives a test of strength to achieve
We are truly made stronger if we surrender and believe
Belief means acceptance beyond a shadow of a doubt
Don't ever doubt God's plan for you and what it's about
Yes, we may try to reason out just what He has in store
And the real story is that Jesus knew it long before
So, before we complain about our crosses and trials
Know full well that saints applaud and heaven smiles
Smiling in joy over the one who repents of his sin
Because sin has no place in your heart where heaven begins
Just as sure, in the beginning, God made the heavens and the earth
He saw that it was good and all of creation came to birth
Should we not ask to be born of the Spirit to start
To begin our life-long journey of love to set us apart
Yet apart from God we can do nothing as we will see
Let's see to it that we unite our wills to His for all eternity
Yes, in knowing that hope springs eternal at best
Can truly bring comfort while enabling the soul to rest
So, don't be restless or worry about your outcome
Because truly by acceptance, surrender and love is where grace comes from
Gracious, then, let us all be when called to mercy not law
The law is only one part of the lesson from which we can draw
Draw near to Jesus, then, whose purpose is to show mercy and forgive
Because forgiveness from the will allows us the freedom in which we can live

Let's live by His commands while placing in our hearts and our minds
Be mindful of the fact that we mustn't be left behind
Pray, then, to remain vigilant, prudent and wise
Because salvation is at hand and don't be surprised
Don't be caught off guard, but always be prepared and ready
By preparing the way of the Lord our feet will become steady
Be willing to sacrifice everything to everyone be it big or small
Then you will be counted amongst the saints after all

Written by:
Nancy E. Willard
October 24, 2017

THE NEED FOR OBEDIENCE TO AUTHORITY

If obedience means carrying out with submission
Should we not yield to authority and its commission?
To commit to ordering one's life in a proper respect
Respectfully speaking order is a trait not to neglect
Negligent, then, to the norms and laws enforced
Brings chaos and calamity because disobedience is endorsed
If obedience describes a trait of easily being taught
Then, teaching should be by example and include right thought
You see, thinking about change is the very first step
Let's step up to the plate with promises kept
Keeping focus that compliance to law means to agree
In agreement, then, obedience can make one free
By attaining freedom our choices become clear
As we follow a path, resolutely, without fear
So, let's focus upon resignation to do God's will
And each time we do so, by surrender, we begin to feel fulfilled
Fulfillment brings a purpose or an answer to satisfaction
And to be satisfied brings contentment and clear action
Acting out of meekness, too, enables one to be content
Contentment, then, is the opposite of feeling spent
Spending time in prayer while asking to acquire obedience
Is the fruit of the Spirt which serves us well while making perfect sense
Indeed, limitless in the ability to yield to authority
Yielding to a greater good which can define your identity
Not to be uncertain of your own sense of self-regard
Which takes courage and discipline in order to safeguard
To protect oneself and guard against loss
Is losing one's soul, then, worth the ultimate cost?

Costly, it would be, to lose our sense of wrong and right
Rightfully so, let's act in a spirit of meekness not fright
Let's try to exist in a world with a true sense of hope
Because despair becomes the tool that the enemy uses
To tempt us relentlessly as he confuses
In confusion, we fail to distinguish and become disordered
And being disordered is the complete opposite of knowing order
So, let's strive to be orderly and be willing to obey
Because acting out of obedience, we can in autonomy stay
Yes, automatically things will always fall into place
When placing ourselves in God's hands and being surrounded by
His grace:

Written by:
Nancy E. Willard

THE MISERY OF BEING A SLAVE TO YOURSELF

When all you can see are your bad habits repeated
And all your energy and money depleted
By poor choices made in buying to an extreme
Overwhelmed by the quantity bringing lack of self-esteem
Left with a situation obsessed to buy
Spending money foolishly which can't be denied
Leaving on hopeless and angry, too, inside
In essence we are called to deny ourselves and follow Christ first
To surrender ourselves completely which leads to a thirst
A thirst for a remedy to the sickness we face
In squandering money and creating waste
A waste of time and talent and treasure is a sin
We can't buy our way to heaven or expect to win
Lest we really try to curb our inner desire
For fulfillment of these fleeting obsessions which expire
Expire not just literally but in reality, create
Buying possessions foolishly which do not satiate
The real thirst in my heart is not for riches and gold
Nor for the pride and prestige that can take hold
I must yield to the Father's will and not my own
To be satisfied with the bounty of graces alone
Only by grace, then, can change occur
When putting all our needs in His hands for sure
Surely, too, deliverance and forbearance are what is needed
Needed to overturn greed and hoarding unheeded
Collecting riches and "things" is not what God demands
Rather He wants us to develop a spirit of poverty on the other hand
We have to hand over to Him ourselves entirely without reservation

Because He alone can feed our starvation
He nourishes our body and soul by His Presence
Being present in the Eucharist in His Real Essence
Should we not, then, seek the courage to change
From our sins and our faults and bring an exchange
To trade off our need to be first and be last
And create a lasting promise and cast
To cast out our nets deep ready to catch
Catch on to the idea that only God's love is a match
Then let's strive for a lasting friendship with God above
And obey His commands with our filial love
Indeed, we are truly sons and daughters of God most High
And when we pray to Him in secret, He won't deny
Rather He'll bless us in abundance for sure
And bring help to those of us in need of a cure
A cure to our slavery to selfishness and sin
Because God is the Divine Physician where wellness begins
So, I pray, dear Lord, for a new beginning to strive
Strive for perfection and keep me alive
To live a life of joy and not slavery to self alone
Because I need You, Lord and need to atone
For my many faults and offenses that are repeated
Often done thoughtlessly by being conceited
Please, then curb my pride and make me humble of heart
So, that I may be willing to make a brand-new start

Written by:
Nancy E. Willard
October 17, 2019

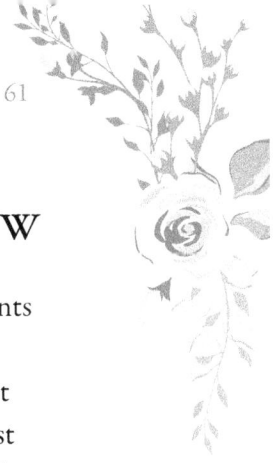

A True Example to Follow

To be materialistic is the opposite of what Jesus wants
Because riches and wealth come back to haunt
Haunting those who seek comfort and status first
Who often fail to recognize true hunger and thirst
As our thirsting Lord seeks to bring heaven to all
Not counting the sacrifice that He makes or the number of times that He falls
If we, too, fall and can get back on our feet
We'll soon realize that we've attained victory and not defeat
A defeatist attitude surely will bring despair, indeed
As negativity runs rampart and to harm leads
What good is there in hopelessness when dealing with obstacles that we face?
When all hope is lost it is to the Lord we should long to embrace
We should wrap our arms around Him and forever cling
To hold fast to the fact that He is our everything
He is the answer to every desire in our hearts that we hold
By holding on to Him, will bring strength untold
We should tell the world of His love so real
In reality, He knows everything that we feel
Feelings get hurt, though, if we fail to be true
Because in truth we are set free and can feel brand new
By this transformation, we realize that mercy is real
And really, it is a fact, that God's mercy, no one can steal
Or take away the peace planted within our souls
Thus, mercy and love take root and will grow seven-fold
So, to grow in Christ, we must always be aware
Aware of the fact that He unconditionally cares
In every facet of our lives and our dreams
As dreams come true we gain in our self-esteem
Oh, what a gift to be at peace—at last
This peace will last as long as we stay steadfast

So, hold on to the fact that everything can be gained
When we lose ourselves in Christ, only abundance will remain
God wants us to have an abundant life as well as security
Yet, He asks for our personal cleanliness and undaunting purity
To be pure of heart—is so necessary, today
Because faith in and fidelity to God is the truest way
In truth, as we come to understand God's love which is eternal
We'll grow from within and not be concerned with the external
Yes, to grow in Christ is not only called for but it is also needed
Because we all need reassurance as well as the belief that we can succeed
Success, then, comes in the forms of discipline and in might
To yield always, to Almighty God, Who, is always right
Let's strive for heaven and the wonders that it holds
Hold on and unite yourself with Christ as our mold
He will then shape us in His likeness and bring about salvation
Which is available to each of us in every land and every nation

Written by:
Nancy E. Willard
November 26, 2017

THE IRONY OF CRITICISM

Have you ever been criticized in your daily affairs?
Or have you been scrutinized beyond what was fair?
In fairness to this question, why do we criticize at all?
Is it really our place to give someone an overhaul?
All too often we criticize people because we intend
With an underlying intention to debase a person and offend
Is it not offensive, when in turn we suggest or imply?
And bring up the faults of others in order to try
To suggest, quite insistently that others are mean
Do we know the whole story behind what is seen?
Upon the first impression we can only summarize
Are we really brief in our judgment of others or do we compromise?
Do we seek revenge participating in a manner which suggests?
Or intend to violate the dignity of those oppressed?
Just as temperatures become oppressive, so, too does the tongue
Are we double-edged in speech when talking about the old and the young?
At each stage in life we must first have respect
To concentrate upon good values without a sense of regret
Indeed, it is regretful not to be able to see every side
Which often gets lost in the shuffle and actually hides
The hidden truth can then remain a choice or desire
Should we not please God, first, by seeking something higher?
To new heights we can climb if cautious and wise
Yes, wisdom in our judgment avoids the telling of lies
Lies only complicate the matter and taint the truth
Truthfully speaking, this occurrence is very uncouth
Awkward and clumsy in manner and speech we become
It is not really becoming to question the motives of some
Sometimes, we should take moral inventory of ourselves as well
Because sometimes we see in others, the same faults in which we excel

The point that we can be a good influence in correcting a wrong
Can be very rewarding and make us strong
It takes strength then, to weigh and balance the facts
In fact, by acting diligently in speech can actually counteract
So, don't go against the grain, if you choose to judge
Be cautious and prudent and don't hold a grudge
Neither begrudge anyone of merit or of praise
Because God's kingdom is ours when we can do what He relays
So, relate to all, in a manner that is suitable to what they deserve
Don't focus on what you can get but work for the purpose to serve
You see, Christ was and is a servant to all
And it serves Him well also, when we can stand tall
Let's then, raise high our standards and be considerate too
Because the measure of how we judge others will render the same for you

Written by:
Nancy E. Willard
December 17, 2017

SERENITY IN SOLITUDE

In these hustled and bustled days of the season each year
Is it really necessary to rush and run around and drink cheer?
Is this our intent to celebrate the here and now and omit the divine?
Are we subtle in our lack of respect of holiness and crossing the line?
Do we stand in line, then, just to get the biggest sale?
And make our goals commercial to augment retail?
Can we really afford all that we want and desire?
While maxing out our credit cards before they expire?
What limit, then, can we put upon ourselves to reverse this trend?
Surely, by discipline and sacrifice, not to borrow but to lend
Lend an ear to God's will when in silence He speaks
He asks us to get to know Him and follow the meek
In meekness we can bring a new meaning to humility for sure
Just as Our Lord was born in a stable obscure
You see, He as God accepted His role of Savior and King
Not in the richness of a kingdom and royal things
But in the quiet and solitude of a humble place
Where shepherds and angels came to embrace
They embraced the thought that this child would be
A person so lowly yet holy in purpose and intent
That is why we celebrate His coming and call it Advent
He comes to this world so unassuming and so small
Yet tiny in stature He will become the greatest of them all
So, let's all endeavor to appreciate and serve this holy child
Not just during Christmastime but also to be reconciled
Reconciliation is so freeing to a soul once distraught
And forgiveness was the gift that Jesus bought
The price that He paid was His life as a ransom for all
Can we not thank Him and in our hearts recall?
Let's make for ourselves some quiet time to converse with the Lord

Because, truly, He is the only gift that we can afford
And He will fill every corner of our hearts with His peace
Which will need no explanation when all wars will cease
Let's find liberty and freedom to become our values to heed
In doing so, we can eliminate tyranny and abolish greed
So, let's not line up in stores with the intention to buy
But rather let's invest our time in God and not deny
Not deny that Jesus is not only the reason for the season and will always be
The cause for our truthful joy and blissful serenity
Because His purpose is to gift us with Heaven so real
And doesn't knowing that this is true hold delight and appeal
Let me, then, appeal to your sense of wonder, awe and peace
Let's put Christ back into Christmas and help Him release
The joy in our hearts that He alone can give
That's His promise to us always for as long as we live

Written by:
Nancy E. Willard
December 25, 2017

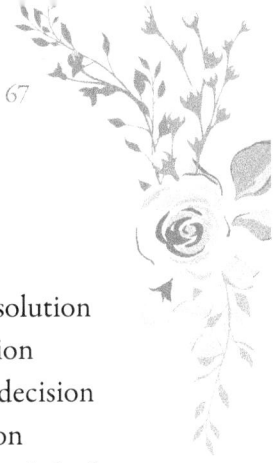

A NEW YEAR'S WISH

It is said that if we are not the problem then we are the solution
The fact does remain true if we make it our resolution
Let's resolve, then, to make it our goal and make a clear decision
And follow with an attitude of clarity and precision
Yes, to decide to affirm as well as to confirm our strongest belief
Believing that real tenacity can bring relief
You see, freeing a person from pain and lightening the stress
Can we not stress that by allaying anxiety can bring progress?
Indeed, progress invites growth, self-esteem and being sure-footed
Yes, putting our best foot forward is where confidence is rooted
Can we consider going back to our roots and what essentially matters
Focusing on the fundamentals that bind us together rather than scatter
Because being separated in different directions opposes unity and cohesion
Can we not stick together and find a good reason?
A reason to believe in and hope for a future that's secure
Rather, than settle for less and be satisfied to endure?
To put up with the status quo, so to speak plainly
Isn't it plain to see that mediocrity is what we face mainly?
To be in the mainstream of progress should be our endeavor
Not to side step good judgment and the need to be clever
Yes, to be quick-witted in some of our choices is healthy and needed
Need we say, here, how many of us has really succeeded?
Success can be measured by the efforts that we make
And making decisions sometimes results in making mistakes
Let's not be mistaken in believing that things remain the same
In essence change is good and reminds us from where we came
We should all, in fact, come to a place with conviction and resolve
To be involved means to be committed to a cause
While, at the same time, not to seek the applause
Yet, we can applaud and praise those who work toward a goal

While having a positive purpose, in mind, as well as having a willing soul
A willing soul will always answer the call to God's will
Because obedience helps all of us to be fulfilled
Fulfillment touches every facet of our self-worth
Isn't it worthwhile, in a sense, to discover rebirth?
To be born again of the Spirit tried and true
Truly, by our Baptism we are called to renew
To once more claim our loyalty and pledge to God and vow
By renouncing the forces of evil, by grace, God endows
Yes, it is our inheritance to claim a life that is abundant
And by doing so, let us never be reluctant
Or hesitant to say: I resolve with all my heart, never to offend Thee
My Lord and my God who loves and created me
In His image and likeness—because He willed
He wills us to share Heaven with Him and be fulfilled
Forever in Heaven with sinners and saints alike
Without any status, competition or any reason to dislike
Rather, in His likeness, we'll achieve cleanliness of heart
While experiencing a holy bliss that only God can impart

Written by:
Nancy E. Willard
January 1, 2018

WHERE HAS DECENCY GONE

Oh, dear people what have you done to society
It has become improper, impure and lacking in piety
Where is the loyalty and devotion for all of mankind?
When we kill for attention or we steal from the blind
Do we put blinders on when it comes to a crime?
Are we deaf to the screams during abortion times?
In time, high morals and standards will be extinct for sure
And life as we know it will pass away without a cure
You see, healing of hearts, souls and minds are necessary, indeed
What tragedy exists when people don't heed
Heed the warning signs of inappropriateness and consumption
Both of which lead to avarice and corruption
Yes, being morally unsound and by dulling the senses
Brings tyranny to the soul and sinful offenses
How much more are we willing to condone what is wrong?
Surely, without cross-checking, it won't take long
To weaken the strong and diminish our strength
Are we capable of change and to go to new lengths?
A lengthy discussion must be had by many here
The many must speak up and make it very clear
We must focus, not in deifying ourselves but in turning to God as our Head
And serve Him alone and feed upon His Holy Bread
His Bread is real food—so little realized when consumed
We're heading for spiritual warfare and will be doomed
Damnation is a choice when we deliberately ignore God and His will
He does not will us to separated from Him but rather fulfill
Jesus, came to fulfill the law and bring mercy for all
One way to call upon God is to pray from your heart
Beat your breast with sorrow for your sins from the start
Go to confession often and polish your soul

With the divine luster of grace and be bold
Dare to speak out about the crimes and offenses done
For Heaven's sake don't cause our children to run
Neither to flee from gun shots from someone deranged
Nor from the abortion clinic where child murder is arranged
The only hope for mankind, then, is to turn to faith, hope and love
With love as the greatest—it can give us a shove
To push us toward decency while depending upon God
For every situation or road that we trod
Let there be peace and harmony called for by all
Then troubles and wars will cease as pride falls
Yes, pride of the wrong kind is the enemy of decency and good
This fact must be realized and clearly understood
If we can understand and acknowledge that God comes first
All other things will fall into place—unrehearsed
So, let's do our part by practicing as a Catholic witness true
Because to say "yes", Heavenly Father, is what Jesus would do

Written by:
Nancy E. Willard
February 17, 2018

AN EXCHANGE OF LOVE

When love is evident—it has a glow
Lighting one's world wherever you go
This light radiates one's feelings inside
And it is from within one's heart we take pride
A good kind of pride which sets you apart
Apart from the ordinary—right from the start
Starting over is far from necessary with feelings true
Truthfully speaking, we can feel brand new
New in the sense that the heart begins to sing and to dance
In step, then, it is our life that becomes enhanced
So improved is the person who shares this feeling
That feeling will last as long as it is appealing
I appeal that these feelings will last a life long
Because what we long for grows very strong
When we give to another a love that is due
Due to the fact that being loved makes us feel brand new
It is not new that people fall in love together
Be it spring, summer, fall or inclement weather
Will you weather this storm which cause much commotion?
By calming my fears with your sincere devotion
Cast away the low points that life can produce
Because we're either a product of autonomy or abuse
Let's never abuse the bond and harmony that we share
Because a love shared cannot be compared
By comparison, then, we must always hold dear
Dear to our heart—this love so true and clear
Will you, dear one, walk that extra mile with me
And keep in step with every stride or degree
It takes patience and temperance both to be kind
Kindness is paramount when hearts are inclined

Incline your ear, then, to these words that are meant
And find meaning in them and their intent
It is my intention, alone, to lift your heart
In heartfelt love that can set apart
By distinguishing between what true love holds
Or to feel unrequited love leaving false hope that enfolds
Quite the opposite when embracing the kind of love that we share
Is one that vicarious feeling that can't ever be compared
Nor can that love be questioned, because it exists in truth happily
Let's ever be true to each other and agree
Agree to never hurt one another either deliberately or jest
Let us then smile and laugh—because we've got the best
Yes, the best is yet to come, my dear
Because our love is precious and sincere
Forever in a kind of rapture, so to speak
I speak of this love, then, because it is the very love that I seek

Written by:
Nancy E. Willard
February 22, 2018

FROM DANCING TO ROMANCING

For just a brief moment I'd like to reflect
Look back at the times when we shared full respect
Respectfully so, I have the courage to say
Say from my heart—I love the way
The way that you glow while on the dance floor
Means the world to me even more
I'll treasure these times and hold in my heart
These memories that bind us and set us apart
Apart from the maddening crowd, so to speak
I speak the truth and will forever seek
To find and seek the very best that you can be
It's because I can witness the genuineness that I see
Let's see to it, then, that we will highly esteem
And lift each other up while holding on to our dreams
We can deal with any concern or problem that arises
And focus upon growth and its many surprises
To bring each other the humor of a situation at hand
And roll with the punches the best that we can
What I'm getting at, here, is the suggestion to grow
To encourage each other in every situation we know
Knowingly being a part of a friendship, not common, but rare
Isn't wonderful to know that someone cares
Let's take care to never hurt one another with the intention
Of turning our backs on each other and not to mention
To speak from the heart a purpose to become
Become the best that we can be and then some
Sometimes it will take some swallowing of pride
While recognizing that there's always another side
Will you walk by my side with sincerity and grace?
Because it becomes very wise to know one's place

Let's place upon each other our highest esteem
And we'll soon realize that there can be truth to our dreams
So, in looking forward to the future, let's always be modest
With purity of heart and intentions honest
It's a good trait to have mutual high goals
And to experience true growth and what it can hold
Let's hold on, then, to right thinking and feelings true
And share with each other a love known to few
Few and far between can accept this challenge and what it holds
Let's together grow in love and watch what enfolds
We can discover that true love can exist forever
For those who take care not to hurt the other—ever
Everything else, then, falls into place
Because we're honest and true while giving each other space
In space and time, I believe that God, has intervened
And brought us together to share those feelings so serene
With serenity, then, as the goal of our friendship
Will you seize the moment and get a grip?
And hold on to the fact that we're never alone
As long as we have each other our love will be known

Written by:
Nancy E. Willard
February 24, 2018

A SILENT DISCOVERY

How often do we catch ourselves saying "I need a vacation"?
Far from our hurried world that we endure in frustration
Are your plans thwarted and seemingly impossible to achieve?
Can we accomplish our goals in what we perceive?
To focus on the present moment and feel that quiet call
Calling us to be still and listen to a voice we recall
That voice is ever present to us especially when silent
And in that silence, we know that we must be compliant
Yes, in confidence, we become refreshed and renewed
By taking a moment to pause and then review
Are we not accountable to God for our efforts and time?
In time, then, can we not look to the very reason and rhyme
Which orders our world creating the opportunity to open a door
Revealing God's full intentions and what He has in store
We are not to store up treasures of the worldly kind
But rather we must be poor in spirit and treasure what we find
This newly found peace can bring us joy and real contentment
Which is the opposite of our own fears and hidden resentments
We must not injure or offend those we pass along the way
Because wayward we'll become if in our anger we stay
You see anger is vehement and destructive as well
Let us well be in check of our pride which can swell
Then swell-headed and arrogant makes us unwilling to hear
Not allowing us to hear our conscience which should be kept clear
Telling lies about others is not just a personal sin
That sin affects all of us and can truly begin
Begin to tear apart the essence of truth that we seek
Allowing us to feel frustrated, confused and very weak
We must not weaken, then, but rather re-double our strength
To become a strong warrior for Jesus and to go to any length
Just as He surrendered His life to conquer death and sin

Let us become brave and loyal and willing to begin
To embark upon the journey that God will direct
As we follow His lead with true respect
Because He loves us with a love like we've never known
By assuring us constantly that we're never alone
By realizing this fact should always make us feel
That we are special and should forever kneel
To worship our God with renewed strength and boldness
As He enflames our hearts, He casts out the coldness
Nor are we to become tepid or lukewarm in our attitude
Rather we must be bold in character and full of gratitude
This very thought reflects and calls for our ability to think
To think highly of God always and not to trust our own instincts
So, let's more often seek some leisure time and reflect
Reflect upon the fact that God deserves our first respect
If we can all discipline ourselves to this theme
There won't be a need to lie or devise any scheme
In taking time, then, to use our leisure time well
Let's welcome our God to enter our souls and there indwell
He will then become all the comfort and rest that we need
And fortify us with His grace in order to succeed
Success will come finally to those who extend
Reach out for the hand of God and the love that He sends
He sends us as missionaries and asks that our lives we commit
And being committed we'll remain until we submit
By surrendering our time, treasure and talent for His pleasure
And we will discover a "peaceful joy" beyond measure
Can we measure up to this call so sorely, needed
I think not, because Jesus has already succeeded
Let's ponder within, in the silence of angels around
And nestle in their wings in the peace that we've found

Written by:
Nancy E. Willard
March 8, 2018

COME HOLY SPIRIT-COME

Oh, greatest sanctifier above all else help me to rise above
Give me that special grace to love you first in filial love
Because when love is born from you there is no end to delight
It becomes the delight of the soul to take flight
To become elevated in the desire to do everything well
Welcoming souls in a love relationship only to foretell
Then by foretelling of a future rich in love yet poor in truth
Because the truth of the matter is that love becomes the proof
To prove for all time the Holy Spirit abounds in wonderful traits
These traits leading us boldly to what demonstrates
Sharing once and for all the fear of the Lord is solemn and deep
Because in the awe of his strength we deepen our love for him with a new
desire to keep
Being desirous to hold fast on to truth and what can transpire
Indeed, Holy one, your seven gifts are a blueprint for life and what we desire
When we can become engaged in life's joys not its strife you see
Our attitudes change and gratitude always comes to renew our life
Renew and enkindle the fire of a soul so deeply involved
When all things fall into place and are always resolved
Let it here and now be it my resolution to love even more
And help win over souls for Jesus just like heaven can restore
Restore the soul to love more deeply and abide in new fruits to taste
For these fruits are true sustenance and not go to waste
Nor should we put off or aside any good deed to carry out
Why any kindness or act of charity can erase all doubt
So, don't be doubtful or silent when asked to perform charity
Because true love knows no bounds and defines clarity
Let it remain clear, too, that love will always endure
Because endurance takes strength and often becomes the cure
So, let the Spirit of the Lord always shine in your heart

And open up the flood gates to his love when close or apart
And by allowing this sanctifier to rule over your heart and soul will reap
upon your being bringing graces sevenfold
Is this not a worthwhile goal to abide in the spirit in love and in grace?
And in doing so will ensure love always in the final embrace

Written By:
Nancy E. Willard
May 20, 2018

HAVING RETURNED TO THE LIGHT

After having been half-broken, shackled and full of fright
To whom, do you suppose, can we turn to, to make it right?
It is our rightful duty, after all, to give thanks as we should
And it shouldn't surprise us that evil is always conquered by good
How good it is to be complete again, like back to normal
Because normalcy is a gift both to the free and the formal
The formula, then, to an awakening of faith, so to speak
Relates to the way that God speaks to us in a manner so meek
Yes, the Lord's words of encouragement, brings enthusiasm, too
Can we, too, show kindness to others, which has been so long overdue?
If we had it all to do over again what would remain steadfast?
Could we not choose to stay steady, on course, for a start?
To start each day in the present moment is surely an art
Because God only gives us this moment to be a part of His time
In timely fashion, then His timing is sublime
He is most perfect in purpose and calls us by name
To stand up for what's right by the gospel to proclaim
To proclaim the good news that Jesus loves us so much
That He ransomed His life freely—to keep us in touch
Touching each soul with His most tender love of His Heart
Which became the most awesome need that He would impart
He knew with all His Heart that love would heal all wounds and scars
If we would just turn to Him and come "just as we are"
He was no stranger to pain, rejection, indifference and hurt
Yet His life was so charged by immense love and He was ever alert
He fed the hungry, He raised the dead and cured the sick
Yet how many refused Him and judged Him as a lunatic?
He was not a mad man, but rather a man who came to set free
To liberate all of us from sin and the pain of scrutiny
Let's all hold on preciously to this gift of freedom which is a release

Dare to be free and watch you love for Him ever increase
He wants all of us in complete surrender to His will
And in doing so, you'll experience the promises that He fulfills
Let's not sell each other short by only a partial attempt at best
To deepen our relationship with Jesus as our welcomed guest
And always remember that He knows us better than we are able
And He calls us each by name to His divine stable
Just as one of the many mansions He provides us shelter from harm
His providential love becomes a strong and sure alarm
To always take the time to pray and you'll never be lost
Because the salvation of your soul is what it will cost

Written by:
Nancy E. Willard
June 3, 2018

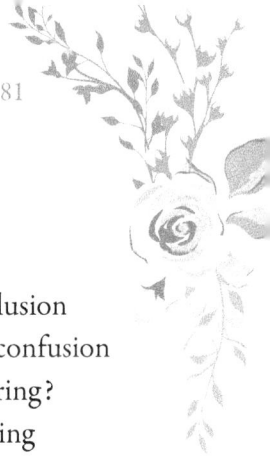

HAPPINESS OR ALLUSION

Just what is the world called between happiness and allusion
While thinking very seriously about it, it summons much confusion
Are we really happy or feel the sensation that it can bring?
Or do we imagine what gloom can bring to everything
In truth and in essence, silencing one's feelings is dangerous indeed
Because when deprived of the benefit of expression thwarts the need
Why do we muffle our emotions so deeply blanketed in pride?
While actually allowing unhappiness and sadness to grow inside
Inside where freedom has so very little room to flourish and grow
While growing apart from the autonomy that we used to know
The answer lies in synchrony of right thought and action
To think positively and act prudently does bring satisfaction
There's so many facts to face, to get it right the first time around
That our knowledge is limited and sometimes in space we are bound
Let it be said, here, though that boundaries bring health
By placing limits, on some conditions, actually produces wealth
Riches, indeed, we can all by high standards within reach
Because, it's all healthy goals we yearn for and beseech
So, truly, in essence we can survive, by the choices that we make
And act in a positive manner, by not making the same mistakes
Though by mistakes we can learn to measure up and value too
Weighing both sides carefully while keeping in view
That God, indeed, is our only source of what matters at all
Receive Him and believe in Him as the author of life as daily He calls
He asks us to trust in Him and greet each day with a smile
Even though, sometimes, it's a tough call and it may take a while
But soon we'll find that smile gets someone's attention
And by paying attention you may have been honorably mentioned
Not necessarily by word, but by some action that did take affect
How affectionate was that hug that you gave—it's cause—it's effect

Let's all strive, then, to be positive on the first time around
And ward-off the "pouts" and that would be frown
And greet those around you with warmth and true affection
And you'll please God and your neighbor and attain some perfection

Written by:
Nancy E. Willard
June 27, 2018

DISCRETION AND GOOD MANNERS

Isn't our own real choice to be polite and kind?
And doesn't kindness often take us out of binds?
It really should be a binding contract to be polite
Because politeness brings and makes contentless a delight
Shouldn't we all delight in the good fortune of all?
And truly celebrate life as a transformation and our call
A call to happiness then is an individual need
We all need to smile more and really take heed
To be vigilant to always take the way to care much
To embrace each moment with a heartfelt touch
Be it that we touch someone's hand or their heart
By this gesture bonds are formed and friendships start
So, try to start each day thanking God and pray
And you'll find that peace and solitude will stay
Stay true to this practice and you'll find such release
Bringing contentment and a joy that will increase
In truth therefore to add to the quality of one state of mind
Thinking positively can lead all the negative behind
What avenue will you chose when facing this challenge real?
It's not to be taken lightly but intended to bring appeal
The type of appeal that delights the senses and calms you down
When all else fails smile and cast off the frown
By being downcast is a real threat to God's intention
You see he desires our full cooperation and attention
And by paying attention to God and scripture still
Will truly educate us to learn and follow his will
Will we be counted amongst the chosen and elect?
Certainly, we are all called to be with all due respect
So, respect all life always from the beginning to the end
And you'll be respected and be what you intend

So why not choose to intentionally follow your dream
Because your high standards will always bring self-esteem

Written By:
Nancy E. Willard
July 10, 2018

THE VALUE OF COMPASSION

What a world of difference when you meet kindness face to face
It warms the freezing and debilitating chill that pain can set in place
Bringing to the heart and body a thawing reaction of comfort and peace
Inviting normalcy of feelings to return and bring release
How loving and graceful you are to me – a friend indeed
Just what have I done to enable this friendship to succeed?
Success does come in so many forms it is clear to see
With its highs and its lows and everything in between to a degree
Yet sometimes it is hard to keep the facts true and clear
And have the ability to know what's true and sincere
Just between you and I – I place you in the highest esteem
Because you so encourage my deepest dreams
Because you let me be me no matter what you see or think
My hat is off to you and I gesture you with a wink
You've experienced my joy, my truest pain
You've experienced my sadness and its strain
Yet you always make me feel as though I am worth it somehow
And seldom question if it is the right thing to know
In allowing me to be myself has had its deepest effects
Because you so often have reinforced my self-respect
Respect, too, is what I have in my heart for you too my dear
What greater love is there than to cling to and to adhere
Clearly and truly as two different hearts meld and unite
Can seldom be experienced as by chance but by pure delight
Rightfully so, dear one, no one can hold the flame to the candle
that you hold
Or warmth the heart by the care you cause my heart to enfold
You go right to the source of my heart every time that Jesus says
Give her my comfort and love and abide in my ways
By the flame you place in my heart every time

God rewards me with His sacredness so sublime
And I pray that I can give you that same love to last you a long life for sure
May our lives be mutually blessed and forever endure
That is my wish, my heartfelt gift my prayer for SURE
Yes, I am sure of one thing that prayers will continue to flow between our
hearts and minds
Because God has made His will clear and does so for all mankind
Please take this poem permanently into your repertoire for as long
as you need
Because there are many hearts to be captured and souls to be freed

Written by:
Nancy E. Willard
July 23, 2018

I Need to Cry Out to You, Oh Lord

My life would be a wreck if I didn't have you to depend
To pray to entrust my life upon your shoulders to lend
Dependent I am on you for everything near and far
You are in my mind constantly I want to be where you are
In heaven with you giving you sternal thanks and praise
Not to have concern for my earthly nights and days
Days are long and tedious when not in your sight
Because I see things only halfway and I am often uptight
So that is why I need to cling to you moments at a time
To love you to hope in you that is my purpose prime
Rarely can I function in thoughts eternal
Especially when losing hope in the eternal
Oh God, you are mighty and wonderous in my search for thee
Will you come and stay a while with me and help me to see
To envision what paradise must be like and what it holds
Holding on to the promise of salvation as we are told
Let me no longer despair in my efforts to walk with thee
Take my heart head and hand and help me to see
See that you are not so far away In a distant place
But rather you are near in my soul in actual grace
By this grace then help me to become more Holy indeed
Let me please taste your sweetness and always be in need
I need you Lord and want to love thee beyond measure
Please come into my heart because you are the treasure
I seek not riches or reward of the earthly kind
To gather dust or corrode into someone less refined
Rather sweeten my life like sugar and honey
And lessen my need for earthly needs and money

Help me to make sense of your will for me in all my affairs
And submit with my fiat to all your cares
So much better I will be when surrounded by you I will be
As you hold me in the palm of your hand eternally
What more could I wish for beyond an intimate life with you?
I will always cry out to you Lord because you make all things brand new
Beckon me please to a life full of holiness always
Let my heart and mouth speak of thy love forever I pray

Written By:
Nancy E. Willard
August 8, 2018

OH, LEAD ME KINDLY LIGHT

When in the doom and darkness so real
All effort and all love bring little appeal
It is not appealing to be constantly in SADNESS
My heart is heavy and beating without gladness
What an awful trick it is to be sad in heart
The pain is growing worse than from the start
How do I start to convey my loneliness of soul?
The apparent split being double fold
I lack the confidence to claim you God as first
That is why I am hungry and that I thirst
Please quench my thirst and isolation and grace me with your presence
Lest I lose Your company and Your divine essence
Don't overthink your thoughts or have despair
Despair is for those who don't really care
Your care and concern should be a prayer to be set free
Free from internal conflict to a large degree
There is no shamed in feeling defeated without a cause
Because in isolation you have stopped and paused
Please stop this isolation which is the devil's world
And bring freedom to me like a flag unfurled
We are not meant to harm or bring harm to anyone else you see
So, I must climb out of boredom won't you agree
To find purpose in life is a real start
And get with the program that you are smart
Intelligent and clever enough to get out of this hole
A place called nowhere—please give food to my soul
To walk and talk of a journey of love as it is meant to be
Be bold and proud of your possibilities
Possibly I can affect the world somehow
By a smile or a nod or even a bow

Poetry you see is not just rhyming in time
It is giving God credit if when it doesn't rhyme
Lead kindly light of your clear Gospel news
That Jesus knew first how to deal with the blues
Follow the Spirit's prompting when you can
And He'll delight you by His grace—we're not second hand
But rather we're first in God's kingdom here and now
Let our knees bend for the hope and grace to let our head bow
Bow to Him not only in silence but in shouts of joy
That is how His graces work for us to employ

Written by:
Nancy E. Willard
August 14, 2018

A LEAP OF FAITH

To step out in faith means to believe
Believing often in the unknown for some relief
It could be the surrendering of the will inside
It could be a form of relinquishing our pride
When pride is at stake what measures do we take
Do we yield to the truth and admit our mistake?
Do we recognize the need to take a step back and see?
That always having our own way doesn't make us free
With freedom, as our choice then, what should we chose?
To take determined steps to win or should we lose
We shouldn't lose hope, however, if change comes about
Because change often brings us to another route
What can determine our course of direction is simple
If our choices have true meaning and our feelings are nimble
To act prudently with wisdom as our goal
Can bring success upon success double-fold
But what should be primary is belief in God and His ways
Because His commandments and love never will lead us astray
Just how can we reach out to those who go via a wayward course
We do so with patience and with kindness we reinforce
You see we're all in the same boat, really, floundering at sea
Being tossed about in waves and by the current seemingly
What seems to often change our course, though, takes faith as a leap
To believe in someone stronger than us and go out into the deep
You see depth of character does not take faith alone
It also means saying yes when we feel that we're prone
Yet in our weakest moments, God and Mary take hold
Because we are their children that they loving enfold
So, the next time when perplexed or in doubt that we are
Believe that God is omnipresent and not very far

He calls us to Himself in every present moment daily
And does so out of His love so warmly and gayly
Let's all then say yes in faith and answer His call
Because Heaven is our calling that He beckons to us all

Written by:
Nancy E. Willard
September 10, 2018

CPSIA information can be obtained
at www.ICGtesting.com
Printed in the USA
JSHW050307300722
28628JS00006B/218